Poet Laureate
of the BBQ Joint

poems by

Lauren Boisvert

Finishing Line Press
Georgetown, Kentucky

Poet Laureate
of the BBQ Joint

Copyright © 2022 by Lauren Boisvert
ISBN 978-1-64662-880-3 First Edition
All rights reserved under International and Pan-American Copyright Conventions. No part of this book may be reproduced in any manner whatsoever without written permission from the publisher, except in the case of brief quotations embodied in critical articles and reviews.

ACKNOWLEDGMENTS

Grateful acknowledgement to the following publications, in which these poems first appeared:

"Open Letter to a Cousin Gone 12 Years…", *spy kids review,* 2016 and "Save a Seat for Me in the Void", *Sixfold,* 2017

Publisher: Leah Huete de Maines
Editor: Christen Kincaid
Cover Art and Design: Jocelyn Hall
Author Photo: Lauren Boisvert

Order online: www.finishinglinepress.com
also available on amazon.com

Author inquiries and mail orders:
Finishing Line Press
PO Box 1626
Georgetown, Kentucky 40324
USA

Table of Contents

Maybe an Artist Can't Be Kind 1

10 Facts about the Poet You Will Never Hear Anywhere Else 2

A Girl Walks Home Alone at Night 3

Deer Die with their Eyes Wide Open 4

What My Hands Wanted to Hold as They Cam Out
    of the Kiln 5

Reading Sandra Cisneros on the Beach with a Hangover 7

I Am the Floridian Sitting Next to You On the Plane
    When You Leave 8

An Open Letter To a Cousin Gone Twelve Years or
    Please Don't Talk to Me About This Poem 9

Driving to Work and It's Still Dark 10

Bramblepelt Take My Memories 11

You and Me and The Machine 2 12

Ted Hughes' Women 13

I Will Keep Your Death 15

Sometimes You Have to Pour from an Empty Cup 17

Simulacra and Sumulation 18

Save a Seat for Me in the Void 20

Maybe an Artist Can't Be Kind

I am not an artist
        but a caged animal
beating at the enter key with my forehead
        until bloody.
There can be kindness in poetry but
                who wants to read a poem anymore?
Catch me in my empty spaces
        doing cartwheels over kindness
            kicking kindness against my heels   until
                it shatters like a Fabergé eggshell.

I have a friend who makes kind art
        but she is the only one I know
        whose art does not disturb.

Who will hang this poem in the Accademia?
        Who will hang me
        next to Michelangelo
        arms draped around David like a prayer shawl.
This will be my "Brooklyn Crucifixion"
        (my name is Asher Lev   and I am an observant Jew)
I allude to works I am reading in school.
            A professor says
                "Maybe an artist can't be kind"
        and I think
"I know of one, but that is all."

10 Facts about the Poet You Will Never Hear Anywhere Else

1. I hold the record for eating the stars.
   My photo is on the wall. I won a t-shirt.

2. There is nothing down past the depths of my eyes
   except for dust and empty beer cans.

3. My secret to kissing is a clamshell tongue.

4. I am an agate waiting to be broken.

5. If I ever hold my hand over open flame
   know it's only because I want everyone in the room
   to think I'm a witch.

6. Everything I do is because I want everyone to think
   I'm a witch.

7. I cry tears of crystal and purple glass.
   Collect my sadness in a jar to display in the window.

8. If a Sorry ever falls from my mouth catch it
   before it hits the floor. It is my only one and it likes to escape.

9. I have never loved a boy as much as I have loved them all.

10. I like to die, but I am not very good at it.

A Girl Walks Home Alone at Night

Sings badly like a lamb
        wool untouched as soap suds.

Her song does not exist outside her body
        song of guts and innardsred dark purple bruise.

On her surface she is a winter lake
          to black-veined marble.

Railroad spikes in her fingers like engagement rings
        blood on her teeth   flurry of dirt and Spanish moss
there is nothing she can't make
with her twig and twine hands.

When there are girls like this we call them witches
        and burn them from the inside.

A girl walks home alone at night
        and the stars make paths for her black high heels
each footstep a hiccup in the heavens.

Makes sanctuary in the steeple of her fingers
        and yellow teeth retract
        rancid breathing stops
        back alley horrors shrink away
in their polo shirts and chinos and nothing better to do at night
but follow a girl walking home.

Deer Die with their Eyes Wide Open

A patch of curls behind your left ear glows in the dark fire of your hair and I run my matchstick fingers through it. We catch and burn like innocent moths. Where are your hands? Where have they been? They touch my skin like a star map, road sign to my secret heart. My ribs are a prison to keep you close though my love is not a punishment; there have been so many who treat it as such that the bones rock shut like clams. Your fingers make a compass to walk the cavern of my cracked open cage. Will you replace what was stolen from me? Will you breach the heavens with your planetary fists and rip my prize from the hands of God? What I have now is a handful of teeth that glisten in the sun like spun sugar. I place them one by one in the mouth of the sleeping doe. She stares through broken blood vessels, legs fish-hooked, once-elegant neck on gruesome display. You are cherry taillights that dissolve into nothing. This is my failure written in blood.

What My Hands Wanted to Hold as They Came Out of the Kiln

I.

Hands   on hands   on hands
what are hands but bowls for sadness to live
what is sadness but a miscarriage of words
what is a miscarriage but hands squeezing too tight.

II.

I have known a man with hands like cattle prods
he falls at my feet   clutches my hollow boned ankles
            and crushes.

III.

A bee comb is a good place to hide your secrets.
Let me say I am made of finger bones
            grabbing at what I can't have.
Read the creases in my palms, see how many children I will have.
Heart line wrapped like fishing wire hooked in the heel of my hand.

All your sweet raw honey is made of secrets.

IV.

Seconds of hands   hours of hands   long hard days of hands
and coming home to your husband's hands
on your waist   on your thigh   between your legs
            around your throat.

V.

Dirty fingernails   creases of a day in half-moons
full moons are saved for the pottery wheel.

VI.

Thumb the slice in the corner of my mouth
I am a four-sided papercut.
        Nothing worth touching is ever any good.

Reading Sandra Cisneros on the Beach with a Hangover

With the sun as a wheel pulsing hot alive
embroidered china blue and yellow
I rock shut as a clam on a green towel feathered with sand
pink flesh protected in my shell
secret pearl of a peach sticky on my hands and mouth.

Hope for Eyes of Zapata on the back of my neck
red skin plummy and warm to touch.

Short legs short temper
but I am drinking blue alcohol from a glass
and pressing my tongue to salted corn
fingers greasy with butter.

Lemons in my glass last night, lemons and peaches
and whisky fermented in an angel's mouth
stroke a lemon down my spine to make spots in the sun
I am citrus and blood and all hearts beating.

I Am the Floridian Sitting Next to You On the Plane When You Leave

Leave the beach with a pocket full of shells a
nd a sunburn   skin red as a newborn
radiating heat in a cramped 737 two-seater aisle
going back to Iowa or South Dakota or
somewhere else landlocked and unsalted.
The sun is different here   red and yellow like a bruise
split open blood orange on our pastel-blue table cloth
fingers combing through palms like stiff hair
tickling the mangroves   caressing the dunes
        like soft naked hips.

And alright,
we're under the same sun   but the clouds
        are our own wonders
bunched up under the sun like children at their mother's skirts
and she smiles on her infinite miracles of gray water and sky.
Sometimes our sky is split down the middle
        black   and   blue
one part tempest   one part blessing.
Have you ever looked up through the eye of a storm
and seen all the old gods grinning down?
Let the Gulf lick your ankles   leave salt tracks
go home   track the salt through your fields
        watch the ocean grow for you.

An Open Letter to a Cousin Gone Twelve Years or Please Don't Talk to Me About This Poem

You'd be twenty-four and handsome / probably / you had these horrible glasses / but so did I / two little bats / blind as river rocks / and just as slippery / I have not grown into my face / so much as I have forced it to look this way / I believe you would have grown into yours / as a foal grows into its new legs / I read Slaughterhouse Five for a class / so of course now I am an expert on death / there is nothing sentimental about me now / I have not thought of you / sat down and really thought / in many years / years that passed like dog ears folded / unfolded / velvet soft years that screamed through the birth canal / my memory is slimy with afterbirth / So it goes / you are dead now but alive sometime else / you are alive on the roof of a shed / you are alive but there is a hornet taking stock of your brain stem / looking for a place to build a nest / As I have said / there is nothing sentimental about me now / You wouldn't like me as I am / I haven't painted my hands in clay dust since I was twelve / I have lost our flattened pennies / I haven't seen a kudzu bush in seven years / I haven't climbed a tree / or caught lightning bugs / or had someone think I was smart / for a long time now / If I had children I would not name them after you / I would not name them after anyone I know who has died / you are too much for a child to live up to / because you are still a child / I was still a child / I did not see your body before you left us / and I do not regret it / even now / I do not regret it /

Driving to Work and It's Still Dark

And my eyes fluttering shut and prying back open
Head tipped back like a devotee
Sitting at a red light
Hands slack on the wheel watching green lights pass overhead
And the full moon like a great swollen eye on a black velvet tablecloth.

Is daylight savings time really for the farmers?
They wake up on the edge of a dog's breath anyway
Stalking the house in a sliver of sunlight like a fingernail clipping
Or floating in the dark with their feet an inch off the ground
Boots trailing flecks of dirt like blood droplets on the hardwood.
I think all farmers have hardwood floors.

I pull into a parking space
On time for once
Finally safe from my closing eyes.

Bramblepelt Take My Memories

And suddenly a rush of nostalgia like moving water
not for Watership Down—I have never read this before
but expect some form of nostalgia for it in future—
but for a series of chapter books about wild cats
I read as a child.

Bramblepelt, take my memories
and throw them to the wolves.

What is nostalgia but the soft down of rabbit fur—
take that rabbit foot on your keychain
and hold its hand in yours like a friend.
What is nostalgia but memory, crosshatched.

Warriors is why I can't stand the sight of a stray cat.
If there is one cat there are thousands
and my heart is gripped by a clawed, padded hand.
This is just to say, listen: keep your cats indoors.

I remember one year my sister's ex-boyfriend
bought her a white rabbit for her birthday.
It had sad red eyes like lingonberries
and long ears flat as deflated balloons.
Its claws grew sharp and yellow as popcorn kernels
but in all the time it lived with us
I don't remember it scratching.
Eventually it grew too big and my dad let it loose
in the woods behind our apartment complex.
My sister didn't go with us, just me and dad
and the rabbit.

What is memory but a nebulous gathering of thought—
I thought I would forget that rabbit
but seventeen years later I am still thinking about it
and crying.

You and Me and The Machine 2

It could be called a room—
two door chicken pen
reducing three people to sardines in the back
gripping the eight-ball gear shift
and throwing it into third—
this is the room where I only spoke of you
letting my words rise to the ceiling like smoke
gathering there like an oncoming storm
swirling winds of words to stream like banners
from the open windows.
What if all I knew of love was you and that car
and what if both are gone now.

This is the room where we sat until 7 a.m.
in a space made of pre-dawn sunlight and blueness
a bubble where I wanted to put your hand on my knee
but got too scared—I would never be so bold
except I assumed you wanted to be with me
so I let you into my room and allowed you to stay there
like a pet or a thick ray of sunshine through an open window.
This was the only room I ever let a boy into
and it stayed that way until I turned twenty-two.

I let you into my room and I'm wondering
are you dead? Are you dead like that car is dead?
I let you into my room with my plumage showing
like a haughty bird and you never said a word about it.

Ted Hughes' Women

may have bent their heads to the same oven.
This is not an endorsement of self-destruction
but only an observation from someone
who also has rocks in the bottom of their heart.
Critics ask "What type of man was Ted Hughes?"
but should ask "What type of women did he love?"
(only one of them killed her child, too.)
((here please note I do not count Nicholas
as an act of his mother but as a solitary animal
of his own making.))

Ted was in bed with her when Sylvia died
the one they rented the house to
the one who had the daughter with Ted's blue eyes
                                    and ski slope nose.
Sylvia's children fit inside their mother's fist
while Alexandra Wevill suffocated in sleep.
Assia was her mother   Assia Wevill with the Jewish hair
renting the house with her husband's ring on her finger
but not her husband in her bed.
Ted's indiscretions did not turn on the gas oven
or they did   who knows   he took his butcher hands
and turned his wife's last journals into scabs.

'Ted' sounds like a gentle man
but his young face was sheet rock
and his old face was a crag of gnarled trees.
Did he touch Sylvia's sweet curled hair
did he fill her jar with pennies
did he pull pins from her mouth
did he unzip her dress like a body bag?

Ariel was not the way she wanted it.
What right did he have to twist her work into knots
and give away her secrets
                (only her entire literary estate
                consisting of one (1) tongue in a jar and
                one (1) beating heart on a silver platter.)

Who is that woman with the Jewish hair
why is she locking doors and windows?

Assia Wevill uses Sylvia's comb   scrubs Sylvia's floors
feeds Sylvia's children   makes love to Sylvia's husband
            bends up Sylvia's wire hanger
while there is a ghost in the walls   beating the
rafters in cadence
I am   I am   I am

In the plainest of language   Sylvia Plath had her own problems.
I assume Assia Wevill was the least of these.

Ask now   "What type of women did he love?"
I will tell you:
                Two swans with broken necks.

Carol Orchard broke the pattern
but she will not be remembered as the others were.

I Will Keep Your Death
    after Deathless *by Catherynne M. Valente*

Winter blows through me
with mouths like shovels;
all of me is skin and bones
even down past the depth of my eyes.

Winter has a thousand mouths
and they all have the yellow teeth of voles,
the sharp of stone on stone,
ragged cut machinery against the soft of you and me.

The dovetail split of you and me
under winter which looms like a general,
snaps like a father's belt,
like a husband's fingers against a tease of skin.
I will keep your death tucked in my cheek
like a pebble, salt-sweet.
I am content on sausage and good bread.

Stroke my heavy fur, brown at the shoulder,
soft and clean as a cat's, a bear's prize.
I wear it often, it becomes me;
your bear, stalking the halls of our fire-made home.

I will keep your death nestled between my breasts
like an egg where it can sleep
by the hearth of my blood and be warm.

I make a home in the corner of a shadow
that falls on a copse of birches.
Here there is no birdsong, only
wheat grass and wild sweet onions
and the creaking of sunlight against the trees.
This is where I keep myself,
and where I keep your death,
in the eye of a needle, in an egg, in my sternum,
warmed by my blood and my desire.

Desire is a living thing inside the birches,
it breathes and snores and hates, sometimes,
when the shadow is thin
and the corner shrinks to a marble
and your death throbs against my bones
like it wants to be born right then, right there.

When you are tired
and my bear shape has gone thin and cold
and there are no more onions or eggs or shadows
you will take your death from me,
crack it on the teeth of a starving dog,
paint my mouth with the sticky yolk
like twelve shades of gold.

This is how the deathless die,
the dovetail split of you and me
under winter falling into spring
the way careless children fall from trees.
It doesn't take long to kiss away your death
with my nails in your cheek holding on,
licking blood in your mouth like new pennies.

Your death is fish hooked inside me,
I will keep it as I keep your secrets
and you will kneel in the snow as a dog kneels
so that I may press my death on your tongue
like a round communion wafer
not stamped with the cross
but with my own red kiss.

Sometimes You Have to Pour from an Empty Cup

You'd be surprised to see me now
how soft I am   like moon sand
nothing like the hard nut shell I was as a teen
when you knew me as nothing more than
a secret Jolene hidden in the trunk of my own car.

I have wine glasses in my apartment
I drink gin out of them   can you believe that
I have a man who drinks gin out of wine glasses with me

I have a man who cleans my glasses for me when I ask
takes them from my pinched fingers and breathes
velvet-soft and slow so all my fingerprints show in bas relief and
sometimes I open my mouth at the same time that he does
so we're connected through our air molecules for half a second.

There is nothing you would recognize in me now
except the smoldering spot of stupid
that somehow seems to linger after ten years
like residue after a lab accident.
That, at least, has not changed much.

Writing this now is like pulling teeth
except I've had teeth pulled and it's nothing like this;
this feels like recovering from having teeth pulled:
lying in bed with a mouth full of blood
and an ache in the ancient jaw where your wisdom lived.

I do not want to write about you anymore
but what else do I have to offer if not my hands upturned
into shallow milk bowls holding the breath of a dog
and a dead black moth.

Sometimes you have to pour from an empty cup
to get anything worth drinking.

Simulacra and Simulation

I press bread to my lips
as if I am kissing my grandmother's cheeks.
    are oil and herb people.
    We are drowning in little bowls.

    In discussion of reality   someone decides to say
          maybe this is just a dream
and I make my crisis quota for the day.
    For someone who delights in salt
    I am frightened of the ocean.

For someone who plays in God's sandbox
I am not a fan of virtual reality;
    what am I if not already a machine?
    what am I if not a copy of a copy of a copy
    only changing on molecular levels?

If the general populous acknowledges a lie
what is stopping it from growing legs and living among us?

    (A lie develops lungs and breathes
    develops hands and squeezes too tight
    develops obsessions and alienates its peers.
    A lie has a meaningful relationship
    only to destroy everything good about it
    with one night and a hundred dollars.)

A truth   meanwhile
    keeps a job for forty years
before retiring to Boca and
    opening a food truck.

Claiming to be woman is my simulation of adulthood.
        As much as I tug on the lie like a fishhook
I am still girl   We are all girl until we pay off our student loans.

Dredge me from the shallow bowl
        lungs soggy and ballooned with olive oil.
When you are only a false reality
        what does that make the bread of you?
        the meat and salt and fat of you
                boiled down to stock   ladled into paper bowls
                    served with a fist of stale bread
                at the soup kitchen.

Simulacrum in the heart of you and yours,
        anatomical reproductions for generations.

Once I read that we've never truly seen what we look like,
        simulacrum in the eyes and mouth,
        hands and ribs and kisses and language

What becomes original
        and what becomes walking talking lie
        with a 401K and a mortgage
        living in your neighborhood?

This is the reality of poetry:
            stream of consciousness
        broken up by enter key.
This is the reality of talent:
            I will be in debt until I die.

Save a Seat for Me in the Void

For two consecutive years
I have seen a dead cat on my birthday.
This has to be an omen, I say to no one, to myself
there is no other answer
        except that there are cats in the world
        and there are cars in the world
        and sometimes they meet and don't get along
sometimes things just happen.

One year before the cats
I started believing you might be dead
because no one had seen you in five years
        or at least I hadn't
and I like to base all decisions on the probability of death.
The probability of death was high
so I decided you were dead
and thought
        sometimes things just happen.

The thing about Boisverts is we love hard
but our secret is we hate even harder
but our solution to this is we are terrible at remembering.
I go out in the woods and carve your name in a slab of ice
and watch my letters melt into girl tears
        lusty with glitter and salt
and they are not in the ice but in my body
shaking the cage of me
and there are cats in the woods sharpening the trees.

Stand your back against red clapboards
so I can throw my knives between all your spaces.
The probability of death is low
        you are alive in my grandfather's house
        with my knives jutting through the walls
        we use them to hang our house keys on.
We have the frozen lake behind us

that I stood on once and never again after that
so I am not accustomed to walking on water
        and neither are you
        I would not like you as much if you were.

The ghosts of two dead cats walk the water
black and white and whole
        clean fur
        mouths pink as Jackie Kennedy's death suit.
I read that somewhere
        she wore "muted pink as the inside of a cat's mouth"
and I think yes, that's true, I have seen that pink
and I sit you down in a chair draped with a bear pelt
and make you open your mouth.
        My grandfather lived in the woods
        but I am probably misremembering the bear pelt
sometimes things just happen.

I take the omen of the dead cats
ball it up like tissue paper
and press it into your sternum like planting a seed
        cup my hands over it and pull out the ghosts.
The cats settle into my grandfather's house
        sneezing in the dust of years
            licking the old glue that holds together his French novels
            rubbing their cold bodies against our legs.
They pick their teeth on the knives in the wall
        and so do I
        and so do you
scraping away the plaque of false memories
until the tragic real gleams in the thick yellow light.

Lauren **Boisvert** is a poet living in Florida. She received a Bachelor's Degree in English/Creative Writing from the University of Central Florida in 2017, and has had work published online and in print with *Memoir Mixtapes, spy kids review, The Broken Plate, Laurels and Bells*, and elsewhere. She received the Excellence in Poetry award from St. Petersburg College in 2014, and was runner-up in the poet's billow Pangaea Prize in 2015. *Poet Laureate of the BBQ Joint* is her first chapbook.

Find her on Instagram @bunny_poems.jpeg

www.ingramcontent.com/pod-product-compliance
Lightning Source LLC
LaVergne TN
LVHW041524070426
835507LV00012B/1795